dear
tiny
flowers

Scott Ferry

dear tiny flowers © 2025 Scott Ferry

Cover art: Leilani Ferry

ISBN: 978-1-962405-18-8

Sheila-Na-Gig Editions
Russell, KY
Hayley Mitchell Haugen, Editor
www.sheilanagigblog.com

acknowledgments

Autumn Sky: "my son screams in the car"

Book of Matches: "there is a time in the evening"

Eunoia Review: "again the doves," "i have thrown two huge bags of mosskiller on my lawn"

MacQueen's Quinterly: "sometimes i speak to myself as if i am a child"

Meat For Tea: "ritual magic," "the threads"

Mid-Atlantic Review: "dear tiny flowers," "tonight the sun sets in its usual fashion," "wasp nest as the body"

ONE ART: "last night the poem"

Pedestal: "when i keep having these shameful dreams"

Pirene's Fountain: "my son plays with a broken bicycle reflector at the park," "sometimes i don't know what to say"

Rye Whiskey Review: "august and there really isn't a reason to be sad"

Sheila-Na-Gig online: "song"

contents

tiny-winged dinosaurs sing sweetly from the trees   9

song   10

when my family says i am always angry   11

things that kill me and save me simultaneously   12

my son screams in the car   13

august and there really isn't a reason to be sad   14

in the carbon-gray morning   15

i see a murmuration of doves   16

my son doesn't cry   17

as we drive through the olympics   18

tonight the sun sets in its usual fashion   19

ritual magic   20

the threads   21

there is a time in the evening   22

my daughter tells me she sees a ghost   23

my son has learned to peel back   24

again the doves   25

sometimes i don't know what to say   26

the poem breaks down here   27

when i keep having these shameful dreams   28

sometimes i speak to myself as if i am a child   29

in the taco joint restroom   30

questions   31

as daffodils emerge in february   32

dear tiny flowers   33

i tilt my head to line up   34

i have thrown two huge bags of moss killer on my lawn   35

my son takes the box of donuts   37

last night the poem   38

my therapist tells me   39

my therapist tells me yesterday   40

to capture the sun   41

my son plays with a broken bicycle reflector at the park   42

wasp nest as the body   43

i've heard   44

The Meadows—mine—
The Mountains—mine—
All Forests—Stintless stars—
As much of noon, as I could take—
Between my finite eyes—

—Emily Dickinson

tiny-winged dinosaurs sing sweetly from the trees

but my yearning is dark with mirrors—
i can take an eye out and throw
it into the blue milk of april

and god answers with feather
with sharp hunger—sparrow wren
dark-eyed junco

there is no death here
except in what i
forget

song

i swallow the organs / and spit up hummingbirds
    i hum a bluefeather / and kill a garden
i grow a testament / and excise a lie
    the trees hang in torment / under bluesky
never are the pains throated / with joy
    inside the singing i try / to remember ease
the body which carries aches / and protects
    i am not the shells / nor the broken bulbs
i remember that god is a light / inside grief
    smashed glass and ants / glint and bite
a humming in the torment / a torrent of promises
    joy a singing in ash / a costume for nausea
little wings spit music / as a consolation
    when i watch the living / i remember to breathe
not much separates the maggot / from the fly
    when i consume the eucharist / blue bottles sing
and the dead wings inside me / flutter

when my family says i am always angry

i show them the inside of my chest
look! inside all of the fires
is the softest light—
inside my heart—
a velvet
ash

things that kill me and save me simultaneously

when my son sweeps a glass to the floor
with his spiderlegs as he wrestles
with his sister and it shatters
and i retrieve every shard
and he says *i'm sorry*
dad

and later i think how nice it would be to
not have to crawl under couches
to clean up for anyone but that
would mean i would be alone
and all this laughter would be
gone

and the silence unbroken

my son screams in the car

because he didn't get to see the giant skeleton
with the santa hat on the way to school
as my daughter calmly scrolls on her phone

i step outside and hear finch northern flicker
and song sparrow call and respond
through the cedar and fir and the low tickling mist

i notice the bright drops on the rugosa and grass
and photograph them as the filtered morning light
illuminates them into opals

i notice my son has stopped crying
and is laughing with his sister in the few
minutes they are alone together

and i think sometimes this earth holds us gently enough
to forget we are skeletons in festive skins
forget that there is a howling inside our vehicles

remember that we are wet and mirrored
as impermanent prisms remember
that when we listen god is

singing

august and there really isn't a reason to be sad

blackberries burst hypertang
blush indigo / overripe berries
slough off like old slang

roses open and open / bees
slip tongues inside filaments
until petals unwing

seabirds scream saltwind
and the sun is an edible god
inside each flesh

the hurt i carry was given
by scared people who couldn't open
any mercy

paint covers or brightens
each of my openings—
black as new air

i can't forgive everyone
but i can melt these
keys

fingers brush iridium
my heart: a small hive /
a noon burn

the fish are clocks / the gods
unwatered and each apology
to myself—

each acceptance speech—
is not at all
sincere

in the carbon-gray morning

when my body is full of dust
all the buildings
tin-boned and holographic

dissolve from the inside—
bodies cubicles snakeplants
wires monitors promises

puff with a hollow cough
and fall like ozymandias
into a wreck of wings

i see a murmuration of doves

breathing its latticed body
above the shipping containers this morning

i step from my car and move closer
to capture it with my camera

zooming in the 50 yards
and praying *please fly over me*

please fly over me
and then 20 seconds later they drift and whorl

directly over my hominid arms
my magic device trained to remake them in my image

but as i reach up i forget to unzoom and every photograph
blurs like an oily palm on a window

and i curse myself as i have learned over and over
to do

i know this whole thing is a metaphor—
the wish and the manifesting

the myth of failure
the lack of satisfaction

when given what has been requested—
the gift a phantom of flight

which flashes and retreats
the grasping and the blaming

the empty sky heavy with
rain

my son doesn't cry

when the sparrow we find barely moving
in our backyard yesterday dies last night

i gently swoop the bird up with a towel
at the instructions of my wife and daughter

and set it into a box full of rags
place a lid on top to keep away predators

and leave it on our patio table overnight
my daughter noticed before bed

it couldn't open its right eye
and it quivered

and this morning my son and i remove the lid
and the bird has become lighter and brittle

a web of soft leaves
a weave of twig and air

and we replace the lid
wait for his sister to wake

prepare for the burial

as we drive through the olympics

my son points to the giants
and says *the trees grow a mountain*

we explain that the trees grow
on the mountains

but what does it matter?
i like his idea better—

roots lift skyward
steller's jay raccoon squirrel moth

ferried up into the mists on swift limbs
a prayer! a great shivering hope

in the thin wind!
a burning! a weeping!

a vast music in our
hands!

tonight the sun sets in its usual fashion

the spheres rotate inside themselves
and then circumnavigate bodies
in curved spacetime

my children splash diamonds
into the fire and acknowledge
the red death

of the light as the arcs of aorta
and carotid spin erythrocytes
through their orbits

and the words which begin in
one mouth kiss another
bacterial and glittering

and the child who began as a
cell swimming and joining
now spins and joins

water to water blood to blood
stars scrape the inside of their
personal gravities

thermal kick and electric stance
i line up the photo so the ray
of sun splits the sound

and enters her as a lasered feather
she of almost 12 rotations
her brother almost 4

so many suns to open each eye
and so many deaths left
to live through

ritual magic

every morning i hold my antidepressant
pill in my lips while i fish out my water

it is a tiny machine which sings to the fish
and allows them to swim peacefully in my water

every morning i swim as a tiny machine
into the air with whales and squids as shiny as jails

as the anger or fear rises in my tide i remember the pill
spinning its bright wings through the water

mackerel and sea stars swish sweet
serotonin prayers through my machine

blank blood of the sky can't reach the me
inside me slowly sparkling its gills

the machine has what it needs to breathe
among fires and terrible flying gods

water takes the pill in and it makes safe
the boiling sky the fish the beaked birds

body now a blind tide—
song a sweep of salt

the threads

inside me connect—
branch to root
birth to death

i grip the thin mercury
which cuts and poisons
if crushed

everything is the same stuff—
light and snapping magnets
a crackling switchboard

and i have learned every time
that my strength is proven
by how gently i can hold each cord

how delicately i can dance
on a toppling boat while
the ocean and sky

revolt

there is a time in the evening

when less of me has to exist
to guard against pain

so what is here can be here—
a wind in the bladed maples

a shaky wraith counting
each earwig and bear tick in my pelt

each deer placenta buried in the rain
and then eaten

each honest god made of hair and wick
in my burnt hands

my daughter tells me she sees a ghost

rushing past our front window
but only out of the corner of her eye
as she is doing something mundane
like wiping up spilled water from the dining table
then flash it runs towards the door
but whenever she looks there is no one
on the porch or in the street

today my son watches television
and i pick up a toy near the computer
and a gray shadow flies across the evening light
faster than a person would walk
but slower than a run and i open the door
thinking my daughter is home
darting from the car

but as the sun comes in through the opening
there is nothing opaque moving
only spring filtered through japanese andromeda
only a still air like the held breath of someone hiding
in the faint reflections and blind runways
a child maybe searching for a secret place
under all places or a woman fleeing
from a familiar evil scared to show her colors

or a man inside a lost photograph of himself
eaten by time but returning to mail that letter
that would never arrive but i can feel an absence
only felt when someone is concealed
within themselves within the fabric of the wind
lightless but swift a continual running
away from the angels which hunt

and hunt

my son has learned to peel back

the green floor of the earth and pull out worms
he quickly places three on top of a rock
studies their serpentine slide
their slow reaching out
through this ache
of light back
into the
dark
i say
wow you
found three
but you have to put
them back they like it
in the dirt and as a gentle god
he sets each one in the soil and rolls
their blindness under the great green weight of life

again the doves

warp and weft above the shipping containers
but too far away to get a crisp picture

as i look up i see a distant bald eagle
shrinking into the western sky

and then i hear the caterwaul of seagulls
i see them capoeira above me on thermals

i video them as they drift to the south
on the hot exhalation of the earth

i think this is for me—this vision
but my body is not different than this

it has its weather and its shrieking angels
and its god which can't free itself

from itself

sometimes i don't know what to say

either the cobalt is too stuck to the nacre
or the retreating tide is too honest
or the singers in the pines implode—
pop! crow to ambergris!
hummingbird to asbestos!
eagle to ore!

my throatbird is a copper bomb!
my words unworded in blue foam!
disaster and lamps! keys and cavities!
my only hope a leaping into what i have
already shed—my shell a dead wardrobe—
my name a leaky disguise

the poem breaks down here

outside the childhood house
paint the tint of lethe

five thousand parking tickets
stuck under the wipers

the windows not broken
the motor still startable

the keys lost as my father's
yells in the hallway

and my mother's quiet
burrowing

there are two kids still
in the back seat

my sister and i try to get
our attention but our

adult selves have other
graves to plan

i think the children
are still alive

trying to be something
worthy of love

when i keep having these shameful dreams

i search for the person   in charge of them
but when i find him   behind the movie curtain
he is also nude   his hair a swath of feathers
he is also late for class   and when he gets there
his teacher says   *you shouldn't be here*
with the normal kids   you should go
to where the others are   he asks *where?*
she pleads to him   *just go before they see*
he stumbles into the hall   and his naked skin
is light in winter   through bare buildings
and all the screaming   swallows in the pines
and i follow him   out into the street
by the loading dock and he   lifts out of his flesh
and becomes the calm   after weeping
and he becomes   a transparent map
of sugarcane and manganese   blue mint flame
curling off his hands   his mother is there
to pick him up   in the 80s chevy
the suffering of the names   is rust
and his next breath becomes   mine

sometimes i speak to myself as if i am a child

you don't need to get so upset
> i say

look! a rainbow over there!
> i say

people don't have the courage to be kind
> i say

through murder and war, god is here
> i say

god is not asleep, my dear boy, god is not asleep
> i say

suffering is what we eat, love is what we birth
> i say

weep all your hungers into the sky
> i say

the stars will dance between the wounds
> i say

laughing is how to make your body a diamond
> i say

hold the heavens open for everyone
> i say

see, you never were alone
> i say

you don't need to tremble
> i say

there are rivers and elms in the light behind death
> i say

home is all of these thorns and all of these songs
> i say

home is a forgetting and a remembering
> i say

home is a black and silver thread inside your tongue
> i say

in the taco joint restroom

my son begins to wash his hands when i try to get some soap
for him from a strange sideways dispenser on the wall / i put
my hand under it as i pull the handle and it squirts three feet
/ i search where it lands and i see my son with a huge gob of
foam in his right eye socket / and then he starts to scream first
from shock then from searing pain / i try to scoop water into
his eye but he just panics more and twists away from me / i
have to wet a paper towel and somehow sneak it under his
shaking hands / i do this again and again as he tries to escape
but he can't see where to go outside of this red blur / finally i
wipe out enough of the alkaline goo so that he can open his
eyes / i get a new cloth wet and wipe again / he says *don't put
soap in my eye dad!* / i say *i'm sorry i'm sorry it was an accident / i
didn't know it would shoot that far i didn't know it would hit you
in the eye / i am so sorry / don't do it again dad! / i won't bud i won't
/ i am so sorry* / which is probably a lie i realize / maybe it won't
be me who does it but he will again be blind and thrashing /
reaching for help but also repelling it / all touch painful / all
trust gone / he has now lived through it once / and when i said
sorry he even eventually said *it's ok dad* / and was able to
drink his horchata / with half a smile and a hard squint

questions

how many times have i bit my lip eating an apple?
how many layers of finger-smudged glass do i look through?
these are not questions but vague complaints—

my cat listlessly meowing as if to assert that the voice is real
that the crystalline structure of bone and spit
and sprinting heart has a function

that the words which project from my mouth
go out and have a plump magnetism gather dew
have an echo back from distant snow-wrapped peaks

that chewing and drinking my own flesh
(even accidentally) is a type of iron-to-gold alchemy
that the windows do not distort by being flesh

that the fish in the salty sea are singing
isolated horrors concurrently
that god is a crow wishing

into a mirror

as daffodils emerge in february

grand shoots reach up—
fire inside mute bulbs

in winter i swim in a white sea
to the sun to a seed

all is sacred in its eruption its zenith
its corruption its return

i know i am caught in the slow slide
back into soil

but i am not my death but all of this—
my entrance and exit immaterial

a great eyeless eye in a bodiless heart
there is no defense against the rushing

all green stretches up—roots explode!
the fire seethes!

this blood a new flash in
my buried bones!

dear tiny flowers

i know you are weeds and i would kill you
without mercy if you were in my yard
but this is not my space to manage
so i find you wondrous
and take photos of you
zoom in on your opalescence—

the hairs of your neck reaching for water and sun
your stamen and pistil your style and stigma
your musical lure to micro-pollinators
you are your own progenitor
in an endless flick of seed and root
and bloom and fruit

here in this world i cannot control
(and i rage against the powerlessness)
you are a testament to a current
which surges and boils in the detritus
which paints the blank grass lilac and white
which paints the carmine mind blank as wind

you are everything which exists
outside and inside the field of chaos and spring
you have won have always won will always win—
every nerve is a geranium bolting in the dark
every breath an impatien pod impregnating
the vacuum

i tilt my head to line up

my windshield tint with the red lights
but it doesn't quite work

as if a forced order of objects in my field of vision
could save me

from a faraway bomb
from a violent contretemps in my cockpit

all the words for dismemberment
keep scattering

vowel shards whistling
the hard c in calliope and collapse

cutting off legs like fragile ls
here i have some letters

i have kept in my constricted chest
i cough them out—

a cake a candle
a tiny coffin!

i have thrown two huge bags of moss killer on my lawn

now most of the grass is surrounded
by oceans of heartbreak gray

yesterday i pulled grassroots with my hands
from my herb and flower beds

along with buttercups dandelions
and other unwanted growths

piled up bark to stop future
insurrections

i realize i can't get grass to grow
where i want it

but it thrives
where i don't want it

i take an antidepressant to stop intrusive thoughts
from overtaking what i have cultivated

i don't know what i am ripping out
by the roots

i don't know what will thrive
in poisoned soil

i am just moving things to areas i have assigned
because then i have an illusion

that anything i do has a
purpose

my body is sore and my fingernails split
but i feel satisfied for what i can kill

and what i can bless
as a god inside these walls

my son takes the box of donuts

over to the table and attempts to open it
as i am still paying

once i get there i unlock the riches
and he absorbs the first rainbow sprinkle

with astonishing speed
next he grabs the bavarian cream

and i stop him get a knife cut it in fourths
let him slurp up the custard with wide eyes

and next he reaches for the apple fritter
and i also slice off a piece

trying to save him from devouring
the entire world

and when i explain what i have learned
about consuming too much life at once—

pain regret and the unavoidable
crash—

why can't i eat all of them? he asks
because we have to save some for mom and sister

is the answer which he accepts with a grunt
but when we get home he grips the whole fritter

and won't let go and weeps and gnashes and coughs
until he realizes he is full and calmly

walks away

last night the poem

wasn't coming
and my daughter came out of her bedroom
because she couldn't sleep

and she showed me her poem
about sitting on the green slide alone
at recess watching the cherry blossoms fall

like gentle snow and unrequited love
and wishing that people would understand her
and the beauty of the cascading white sky

my therapist tells me

be gentle on yourself and i almost laugh
but i say *ok i'll work on it*

but really it's like putting a man disguise
on a bear and teaching him to sing

and then telling the bear he sounds great
the costume is not fooling anyone

and the bear is now a man
in a bear carcass

afraid of his own
voice

my therapist tells me yesterday

that i can't control everything that i feel is unfair
and that is why i have been suffering

in my head i yell
why does everyone underestimate me?

and then i plead to myself
you want me to just give up?

and then i say out loud
i think it helps me feel safe

i want to know that i have at least tried
she responds that the situation always

is more complex than we can see
and i see myself as a speck of meat

on a window screaming and spitting
at all of the fires—

the body the earth the billions of stars—
dancing a slow burning

waltz

to capture the sun

i have to swim down
where there is no light

lay my blistered skin
on the fire coral

remember what hope is—
draw a schematic

of hydrogen rapturing
to helium

of all my used parts
sloughing off in the frenzy

and a brightness
erupting

like a weightless
nostalgia

my son plays with a broken bicycle reflector at the park

says it's a puzzle so i pocket
the tangerine shards and bring them home

but when we try to put them together
there are too many missing

no way to fit sharpness to sharpness
not even enough to know the size of the circle

and he sighs in disappointment
as we shift the pieces we have in our hands—

severed words torn maps cut tableaus—
and try to create some wholeness

and i want to tell him that no one is ever given
the whole mosaic at once

but we have to pretend we understand
pretend we are satisfied

hoard every persimmon sliver
place them carefully with all of the others

and wait

wasp nest as the body

everything has a little ghost
inside of it—

the paper and spit
surrounding

a hundred eyes—
a hundred wings

i've heard

you are supposed to save yourself
returning to your younger self
the moment you stopped believing
in god

the adult you appears through the wall
a savior weeping at the sight of your wounds
but the child you bites your lip
and hisses

blood from your own face under your nails
and rebukes the approaching intruder
with a chest full of chlorophyll
and grace

young breath metered and sure
under the comets and fires
your name grips the house
as it explodes

your fingers begin the record again
your words slide across a white pain
your voice a holy thing
in the flame

Sheila-Na-Gig Editions